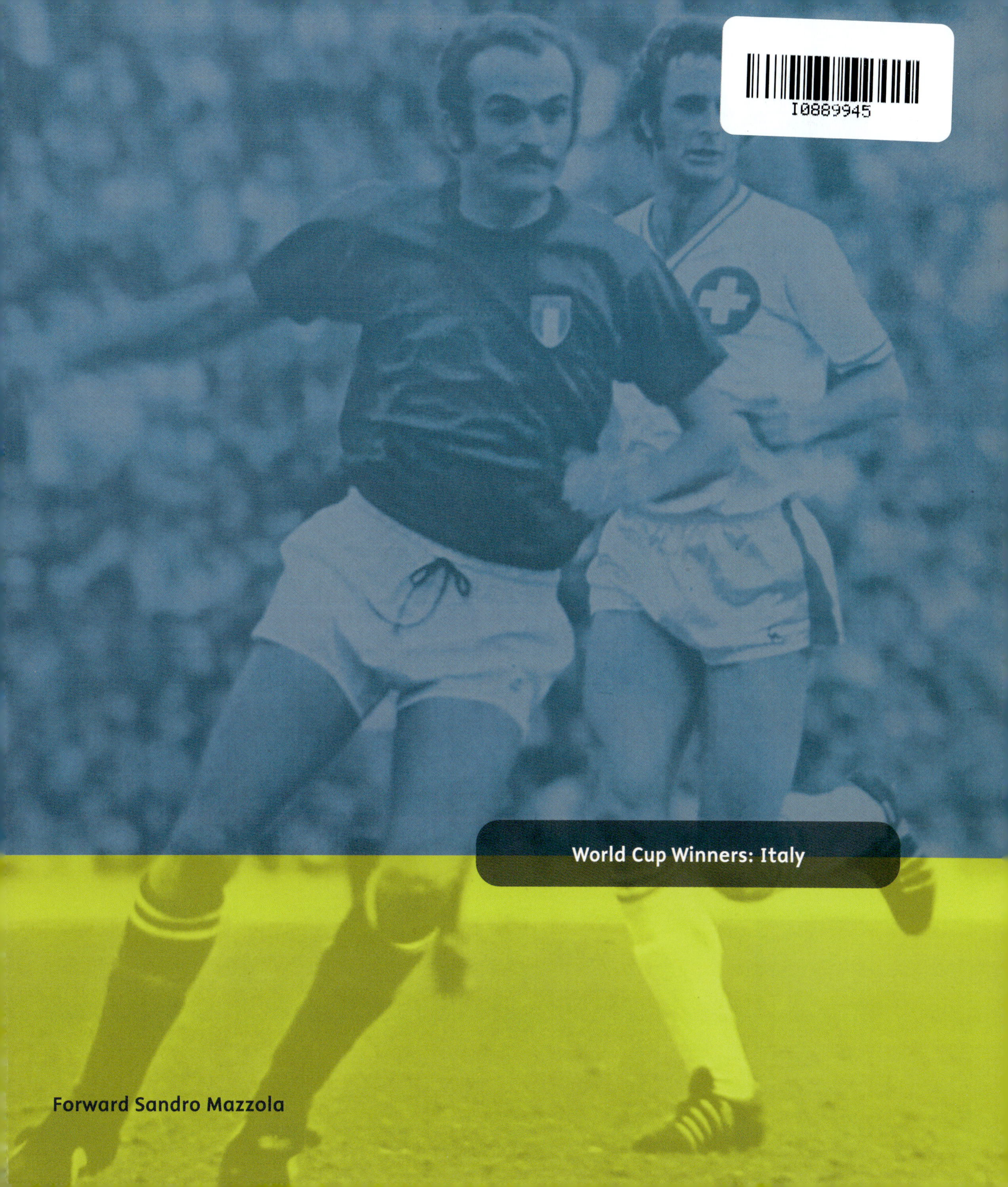

World Cup Winners: Italy

Forward Sandro Mazzola

Midfielder Andrea Pirlo

WORLD CUP WINNERS

ITALY

JAMES BARRY

CREATIVE SPORTS

CREATIVE EDUCATION / CREATIVE PAPERBACKS

Published by Creative Education and Creative Paperbacks
P.O. Box 227, Mankato, Minnesota 56002
Creative Education and Creative Paperbacks are imprints of
The Creative Company
www.thecreativecompany.us

Book design by Blue Design (www.bluedes.com)

Images by Getty Images/Alessandro Sabattini, 19, Claudio Villa, 5, Image Photo Agency, cover, 7, Jerome Prevost, 6, Luca Rossini/NurPhoto, 20, Mark Leech/Offside, 3, 10, 16, Richard Sellers/Allstar, 2, Steve Powell, 15; Unsplash/Rebe Adelaida, 9; Wikimedia Commons/Biser Todorov, 24, public domain, 1, 4, 12
Every effort has been made to contact copyright holders for material reproduced in this book. Any omissions will be rectified in subsequent printings if notice is given to the publisher.

Library of Congress Cataloging-in-Publication Data
Names: Barry, James (Author of children's books), author.
Title: Italy / James Barry.
Description: Mankato, Minnesota : Creative Education and Creative Paperbacks, 2026. | Series: Creative sports. World Cup winners | Includes index. | Audience: Ages 7–10 | Audience: Grades 2–3 | Summary: "Italy has won four FIFA World Cups-second only to soccer giant Brazil! This elementary title follows the "Azzurri" through thrilling soccer action as they seek a fifth FIFA World Cup"– Provided by publisher.
Identifiers: LCCN 2024046139 (print) | LCCN 2024046140 (ebook) | ISBN 9798889896036 (library binding) | ISBN 9781682777695 (paperback) | ISBN 9798889896838 (ebook)
Subjects: LCSH: Soccer–Italy–History–Juvenile literature. | World Cup (Soccer)–History–Juvenile literature.
Classification: LCC GV944.I8 B377 2026 (print) | LCC GV944.I8 (ebook) | DDC 796.334/6680945–dc23/eng/20241121
LC record available at https://lccn.loc.gov/2024046139
LC ebook record available at https://lccn.loc.gov/2024046140

Printed in India

Goalkeeper Gianluigi Buffon

Left-back Paolo Maldini

CONTENTS

Home of the Team

Italy is a country in southern Europe. Its capital is Rome. It's one of the world's oldest great cities. Italy has more than 3,000 museums.

Soccer is by far the most popular sport in Italy. The whole country comes together to support the national team. It's one of the few teams to have won the World Cup. The World Cup is a worldwide soccer tournament. Countries make teams of their best players. Every four years, they compete to become world champion.

ITALY

Attacking midfielder Roberto Baggio

Team Traditions

The Italy national team is known as the "Azzurri" (the "Blues") for its blue jersey. The team is known for its defensive playstyle. Italy's coaches have built many great defenses over the years. Fans go to matches dressed in team colors. Some of them wave flags and sing team songs for the whole 90 minutes. Germany, France, and Brazil are some of Italy's **rivals**.

Forward Angelo Schiavio

Team History

The 1930s were the first great years for Italian soccer. Coach Vittorio Pozzo led the team. Italy won the first World Cup it entered in 1934. It beat Czechoslovakia 2–1 in extra time. **Forward** Angelo Schiavio scored the winning goal in the 95th minute.

The Azzurri defended the title in 1938. They beat Hungary 4–2 to win their second straight World Cup. Italy is the only team to win two World Cups under the same coach.

Italy made its next World Cup final in 1970. But it lost to Brazil. It wasn't until 1982 that Italy won its third World Cup. It beat West Germany 3–1. The team was captained by goalkeeper Dino Zoff. He is still the oldest winner of the World Cup, at over 40 years old. Forward Paolo Rossi scored six goals in the tournament. He won the **Golden Ball**.

Italy made another World Cup final in 1994. But it lost to Brazil. It was the first World Cup decided by penalty kicks. It was a heartbreaking loss for Italy.

The team celebrates its third World Cup win, 1982.

Centre-back Fabio Cannavaro in the 2006 World Cup

The Azzurri bounced back at the 2006 World Cup. They made it to another final. They faced a great France team. It came down to penalty kicks again. This time, Italy secured the victory. It was its fourth World Cup.

Team Stars

Italy has had many great stars in its history. Giuseppe Meazza led the team to its back-to-back World Cups in the 1930s. He won the Golden Ball in 1934. Gianni Rivera won the **Ballon d'Or** in 1969. His nickname was the "Golden Boy." He made his major start in soccer at age 15. Roberto Baggio was a legendary attacking midfielder. He is the only Italian to score in three World Cups.

Striker Luigi Riva (left) and attacking midfielder Gianni Rivera (right)

Midfielder Nicolo Barella

Fabio Cannavaro helped lead Italy to its fourth World Cup in 2006. He is the only defender to win the World Player of the Year award. **Playmaker** Andrea Pirlo was known for his creativity. Gianluigi Buffon is one of the greatest goalkeepers of all time. He played 176 matches for Italy. Midfielder Nicolo Barella is one of Italy's best players today. Fans hope he can help Italy win another World Cup soon.

About the Italy National Team

First year: 1910

Team colors: Savoy blue, dark blue, white

Home stadium: Stadio Olimpico

WORLD CUP VICTORIES:

1934, 2–1 over Czechoslovakia

1938, 4–2 over Hungary

1982, 3–1 over West Germany

2006, 1–1, defeated France 5–3 in penalties

TEAM WEBSITE:

https://www.figc.it/en/national-teams/azzurri/national-team/team/

Glossary

Ballon d'Or — an award given every year to the world's best soccer player

forward — a player who plays near the opposing team's goal and is responsible for scoring

Golden Ball — an award given to the best player in the World Cup

playmaker — a player who controls the flow of play and makes passes leading to goals

rival — a team that plays extra hard against another team

The Italy national team, 2012

Index